THE SONGS OF GILBERT & SULLIVAN FOR UKULELE

Linda Ronstadt and Rex Smith
Pirates of Penzance - Television Adaptation - 1983

ARRANGED BY
DICK SHERIDAN

 To access audio, visit:
www.HalLeonard.com/MyLibrary
Enter Code
4839-1804-6804-8432

Design & Typography by Roy "Rick" Dains
FalconMarketingMedia@gmail.com

ISBN 978-1-57424-326-0

THE SONGS OF GILBERT & SULLIVAN FOR UKULELE

Song Listing

A Policeman's Lot Is Not a Happy One
(The Pirates of Penzance) 12

A Wand'ring Minstrel
(The Mikado) 14

Captain of the Pinafore
(H.M.S. Pinafore) 16

I'm called Little Buttercup
(H.M.S. Pinafore) 18

I've Got a Little List
(The Mikado) 22

If You Give Me Your Attention
(Princess Ida) 26

Model of a Modern Major-General
(The Pirates of Penzance) 28

My Object All Sublime
(The Mikado) 33

Oh, A Private Buffoon
(The Yeomen of the Guard) 34

Poor Wand'ring One
(The Pirates of Penzance) 38

Taken from a County Jail
(The Mikado) 40

The Flowers that Bloom in the Spring
(The Mikado) 42

The Moon and I
(The Mikado) 44

There Is Beauty in the Bellow of the Blast
(The Mikado) 46

Tit-Willow
(The Mikado) 50

We Sail the Ocean Blue
(H.M.S.Pinafore) 52

When I, Dear Friends, Was Called to the Bar
(Trial by Jury) 56

When I Was a Lad
(H.M.S. Pinafore) 60

When I Went to the Bar
(Iolanthe) 62

When You're Lying Awake
(Iolanthe) 64

Whene'er I Spoke
(Princess Ida) 68

THE AUTHOR REFLECTS

"*Was there ever a time when the joyous melodies, magnificent orchestration, clever lyrics and topsy-turvy plots of Gilbert and Sullivan were not spinning around in my head …*"

My friend and I sat high up in one of the balcony's last rows. The stage far below seemed the size of a postage stamp. I had been assured that I would like what was coming, and that proved an understatement. The houselights dimmed, there was a ripple of applause as the conductor rose from the orchestra pit and bowed to the audience, and then it began: the most glorious, liveliest music I had ever heard, and it literally took my breath away! It was a Gilbert and Sullivan comic operetta. The name of the show eludes me now after a hiatus of probably 50 years, but not the memory. Even though the actors from our distance appeared no bigger than an inch, it was magical – the orchestra, the singing, the dialogue, the costumes, the scenery.

I was no stranger to a Gilbert and Sullivan performance, but this was the first time I had heard a professional cast in one of New York City's major Broadway theaters. Many of the songs were familiar. There had been amateur high school productions, community playhouses, school choruses and music classes – all enjoyable in their own way – but nothing rivaled the experience of a real Gilbert and Sullivan comic opera as it was intended to be presented.

In time, there were other professional performances by touring and repertory companies that continued to give full force to the brilliance of this unique collaboration of composer and dramatist. Long after the curtains came down and the theaters darkened, I'd find myself in unguarded moments whistling or humming one of Sullivan's tuneful melodies, while a line or a lyric from any number of Gilbert's humorous songs would be running through my mind.

Scene from "The Pirates of Penzance"

A.S. SEER NEW YORK
COPYRIGHT, 1880

Much of my initial appreciation for Gilbert and Sullivan came from a borrowed reel-to-reel tape that sampled selections from most of their productions. Before returning the tape which I was privileged to keep for many years, I listened to it over and over until I knew every song and might well have slipped in if asked as an understudy. Although I didn't know the opera plots from which the songs were taken, the melodious scores and lyrics were far more than enough for total enjoyment.

To augment the listening experience I acquired recordings of my own – complete scores of many of the operas – and seized every opportunity to hear live performances both amateur and professional.

Truth be told, the first exposure to Gilbert & Sullivan really came from my sister who could play simplified piano arrangements of "We Sail The Ocean Blue" and "I'm Called Little Buttercup" both from H.M.S. Pinafore. Over the years I added my own favorites and found how easily they could be adapted to the ukulele. It didn't take much coaxing to bring out the uke and accompany myself singing a chorus of "A Policeman's Lot" from "The Pirates Of Penzance" or "I've Got A Little List" from The Mikado.

I guess it could be said that arranging this book was DESTINY. Certainly preparation of no other songbook for the ukulele has given me more enjoyment and satisfaction. Knowing so many Gilbert and Sullivan songs has helped, but there were still challenges in analyzing original scores, deciphering the harmonies, and often transposing songs to fit the range of the ukulele.

If the songs are unfamiliar, listen to the online audio then try to play the chords and the tablature. If you're an unsure singer, matching your voice pitch to the tab will help. Don't be daunted by unfamiliar chord shapes. They will be repeated often, and a little effort in deciphering them at first will bring long-term results.

What a pleasure it is to share this collection with you now, and I hope you find the same magic in these lively songs and humorous lyrics that have fascinated me for so long. My hope is that you'll make these songs part of your own repertoire and savor the fun and enduring beauty contained in each. And if you're unfamiliar with the operas from which they are drawn, these songs will hopefully encourage you to seek them out and find the delightful experience they'll bring. You've a wonderful treat in store.

So then, let's now dim the houselights, raise the curtain, and have your well-tuned uke at the ready. ***The show is about to begin.***

GILBERT & SULLIVAN: AN INTRODUCTION

A wand'ring minstrel I,
A thing of shreds and patches,
Of ballads, songs, and snatches,
And dreamy lullaby!

- from **The Mikado**

It is probably safe to say that at any moment in the English speaking world and beyond at least one of Gilbert and Sullivan's comic operas is in production. The popularity of their prodigious output has never waned in almost 150 years. Repertory companies of professional actors, community playhouses of inspired amateurs, scholastic performances from grade school to college – all have kept the glorious madcap world of Gilbert and Sullivan alive and well.

The collaborative talent of Arthur Sullivan's brilliant scores and William S. Gilbert's ingeniously clever lyrics and librettos know few equals in the history of the musical theater. It is held and with good reason that two of the most significant contributions to stages on both sides of the Atlantic are Shakespeare and Gilbert and Sullivan.

It was in 1871 that the team was first paired in a rather hastily prepared Christmas offering called Thespis, but it wasn't until four years later at the urging of impresario Richard D'Oyly Carte that the partnership was again united. D'Oyly Carte wanted a comic opera, Gilbert had already prepared an unproduced libretto, and recalling the pair's input with Thespis, Sullivan was again contacted to score the music. The result was Trial by Jury and it achieved immediate success.

At the urging of D'Oyly Carte the team was encouraged to continue their collaboration, the result of which was fourteen comic operas

produced on an almost annual basis over a span of twenty-five years.

The first three of these (The Sorcerer, H.M.S. Pinafore, and The Pirates of Penzance) were presented at the Opéra Comique Theater leased by Carte in the Strand district of London. But Carte wanted a venue dedicated exclusively to light opera and Gilbert and Sullivan

Caricature of Gilbert & Sullivan

Victorian-era London.

performances, and with this end in mind he commissioned a new theater to be built called the Savoy. It was an elaborate masterpiece of elegant architecture, the first theater ever to have electric lights – but with a gas backup, just in case. It opened in 1881 with the production of the highly successful Mikado. Performances produced there soon became known as the Savoy Operas with players and fans becoming known as Savoyards, just as they are today.

A three-way partnership of D'Oyly Carte, Gilbert and Sullivan had been formed under the name of the D'Oyly Carte Opera Company. It was an ideal match. Carte was the promoter and shrewd business manager, while Gilbert and Sullivan were given complete artistic license and control over their operas. The company remained intact for many years continuing to stage Savoy Operas until it was discontinued in 1988. Several revisions followed, one from 1988 until 2003, and then another in 2013.

Products of the formal Victorian age and despite

their long association, Gilbert and Sullivan never addressed each other by their first name. Sullivan was knighted by Queen Victoria which may have rankled Gilbert until he too was later knighted by the Queen's son following her passing. Sullivan, despite painful bouts of kidney stones, enjoyed the good life and his prosperity. There were long vacations in Italy, high society, and the gaming table diversions of Monte Carlo. Apparently he was something of a procrastinator holding off composing until the last possible minute when pressure was on to complete the score of the current production. It is somewhat lesser known that Sullivan composed the well-known hymn "Onward Christian Soldiers." At the time of his brother Fred's passing, he also wrote the song "The Lost Chord" which was immensely popular in its day. Sullivan's brother had appeared in the leading role of Trial by Jury, and although an architect by trade, he was acknowledged to be a fine actor with a promising stage career.

Unlike Sullivan, Gilbert was always a step ahead, working on the book of a new opera

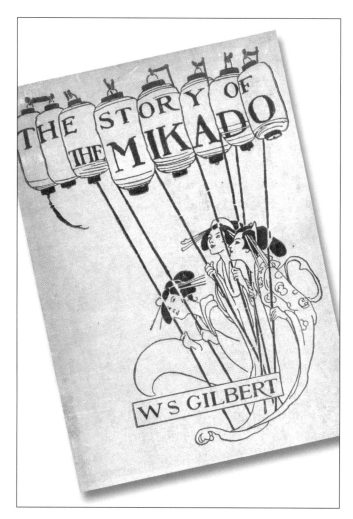

while the current one was still in rehearsal. He was the consummate perfectionist. He had an amazing grasp of the English language and a seemingly inexhaustible vocabulary. His dialogues and rhyming lyrics are nothing but ingenious. He was involved with every aspect of theater production and even had a mock-up at home of the stage so he could envision scenery and the positioning of actors. He too enjoyed the prosperity that came from success; there were yachts and a grand home on estate surroundings. Sadly, a lake on his property brought his demise as he tried to save from drowning a young woman who had fallen in the water. He suffered a heart attack and died at the age of 74. Sullivan predeceased him by ten years and passed away in 1900 at the early age of 58.

All was not always compatible with the troika of D'Oyly Carte, Gilbert and Sullivan. There were disagreements about production, Sullivan's preference for "high class" music, and even a law suit initiated by Gilbert over who should make payment for extravagant new theater carpeting.

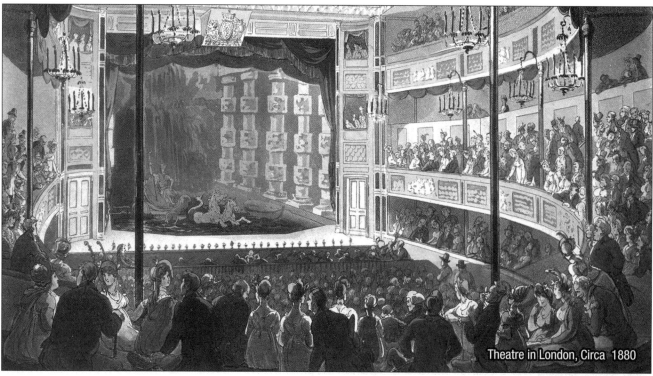

Theatre in London, Circa 1880

It should be mentioned that Gilbert had legal training and had been admitted to the bar. This is reflected in so many references in his writing to the legal profession with its judges, juries and civil miscreants.

For all of this, the end result is the incomparable contribution to the musical stage of Gilbert and Sullivan and their partner D'Oyly Carte. Their evergreen legacy continues just as fresh and vibrant today as it was more than a century ago. Noteworthy too is the considered opinion of many musicologists that Sullivan's works greatly influenced the early 20th century American musical stage, including George Gershwin, Rodgers with Hart and Hammerstein, and Lerner and Loewe.

It is hoped that if you are not already a "Savoyard" that you now will become one. What fun and unlimited enjoyment await you in the songs that follow arranged now for the first time for the ukulele. And, of course, in the broader world there are full-scale theater productions to fill your lives with laughter, scenic beauty, powerful orchestration, and the merry madness that only Gilbert and Sullivan can bring.

For special enjoyment, the reader is directed to check out the many movies and recordings of Gilbert and Sullivan operettas available at libraries, book stores, and for purchase online. Also recommended are the performances ready for viewing on YouTube. Among these is beautiful doe-eyed Linda Ronstadt's "Poor Wand'ring One" from the 1980's NY Central Park production of The Pirates of Penzance. Martyn Green's high-speed patter songs like the unforgettable "Model of a Major-General" left his audiences breathless. Even performances by Groucho Marx and Monty Python's Eric Idle are added to the mix. Notable is lovely Valerie Masterson with her shy coquettish furtive glances singing "The Moon and I" as Yum-Yum in the 1966 film version of The Mikado. Another delightful rendition of this song can be seen on the informal video clip of soprano Alexandra Sanfilippo.

They're all there on recordings, film, television, and the computer with so many more wonderful performances of individual songs, chorus selections, scenes, and entire operas.

GILBERT & SULLIVAN OPERAS & THEIR SONGS

H.M.S. PINAFORE

    Captain of the Pinafore
    I'm Called Little Buttercup
    We Sail the Ocean Blue
    When I Was a Lad

IOLANTHE

    When I Went to the Bar
    When You're Lying Awake

THE MIKADO

    A Wand'ring Minstrel
    I've Got a Little List
    My Object All Sublime
    Taken from a County Jail
    Tit-Willow
    The Flowers that Bloom in the Spring
    The Moon and I
    There Is Beauty in the Bellow of the Blast

THE PIRATES OF PENZANCE

    A Policeman's Lot Is Not a Happy One
    Model of a Modern Major-General
    Poor Wand'ring One

PRINCESS IDA

    If You Give Me Your Attention

THE YEOMEN OF THE GUARD

    Oh, A Private Buffoon

TRIAL BY JURY

    When I, Dear Friends, Was Called to the Bar

A Chronology of GILBERT and SULLIVAN'S MOST FAMOUS OPERAS

1875
Trial by Jury

1877
The Sorcerer

1878
H.M.S Pinafore
(or The Lass that Loved a Sailor)

1879
The Pirate of Penzance
(or The Slave of Duty)

1881
Patience
(or Bunthorne's Bride)

1882
Iolanthe
(or The Peer and the Peri)

1884
Princess Ida
(or Castle Adamant)

1885
The Mikado
(or The Town of Titipu)

1887
Ruddigore
(or The Witches Curse)

1888
Yeomen of the Guard
(or The Merryman and His Bride)

1889
The Gondoliers
(or The King of Baratara)

NOTE FOR BARITONE UKULELE PLAYERS

For Baritone Ukuleles Tuned DGBE:

TO MATCH WITH UKES TUNED gCEA:
1. Play standard notes, chord symbols (letter names) and the CD.
2. Do not play the tablature or chord diagrams.

TO PLAY THE BARITONE UKE BY ITSELF:
1. Play the tablature and chord diagrams.
2. Do not play standard notes or chord symbols (letter names), diagrams or the CD.
3. To play using standard notes, follow the directions for matching ukes tuned to gCEA.

FOR gCEA UKES ACCOMPANYING A BARITONE:
1. If baritone is playing standard notes, play everything as written.
2. If baritone is playing tab and the chord diagram, convert the chord symbol (letter name) that is shown as follows:

A chord changes to an E chord
Bb chord changes to an F chord
C chord changes to a G chord
D chord changes to an A chord
E chord changes to a B chord
F chord changes to a C chord
G chord changes to a D chord

A Policeman's Lot
Is Not a Happy One

Ukulele tuning: gCEA

GILBERT & SULLIVAN

2. When the enterprising burglar's not a -burgling (not a-burgling),
    When the cut-throat isn't occupied in crime ('pied in crime),
    He loves to hear the little brook a-gurgling (brook a-gurgling)
    And listen to the merry village chime (village chime).
    When the coster's finished jumping on his mother (on his mother),
    He loves to lie a-basking in the sun (in the sun).

    Chorus

A Policeman's Lot

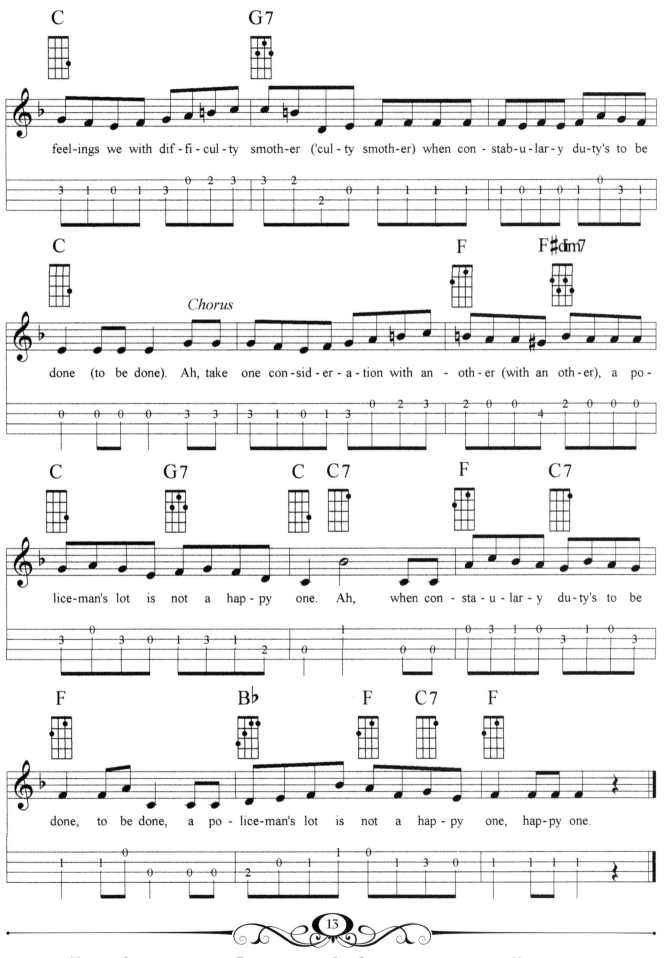

A Wand'ring Minstrel

Ukulele tuning: gCEA

GILBERT & SULLIVAN

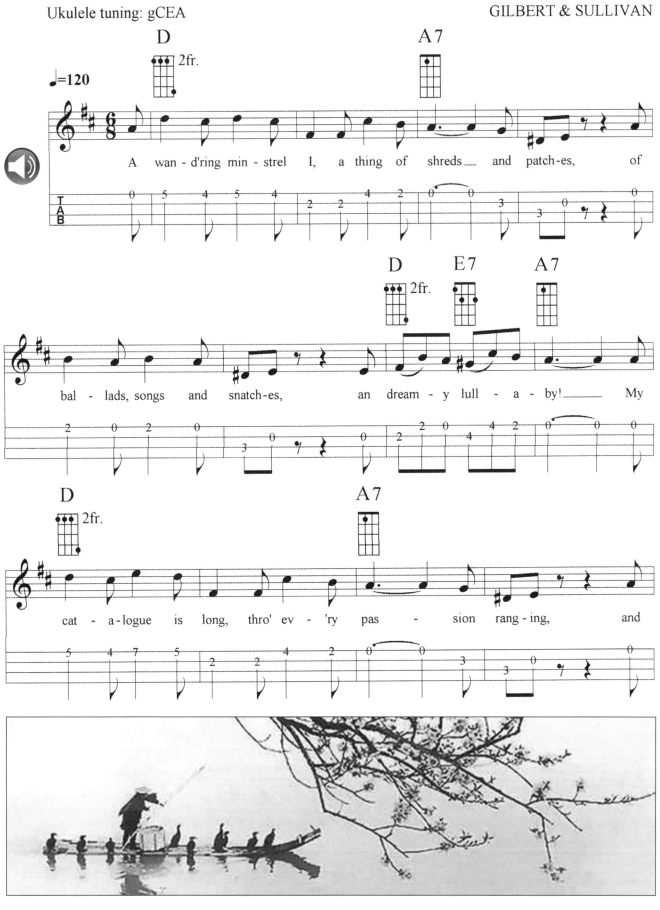

A wan-d'ring min-strel I, a thing of shreds___ and patch-es, of

bal-lads, songs and snatch-es, an dream-y lull-a-by!___ My

cat-a-logue is long, thro' ev-'ry pas-sion rang-ing, and

A Wand'ring Minstrel

I am the Captain of the Pinafore

Ukulele tuning: gCEA

GILBERT & SULLIVAN

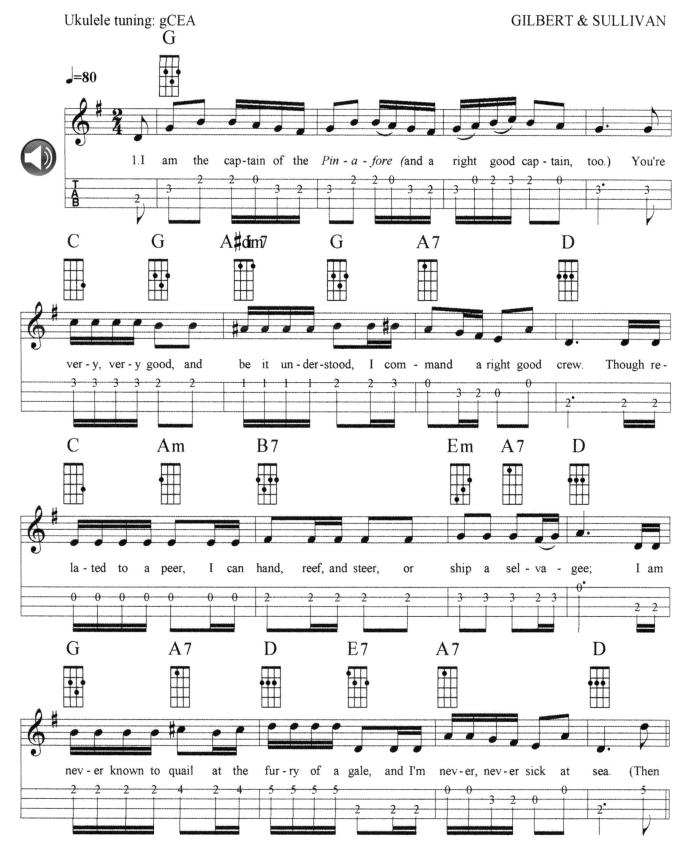

CAPTAIN OF THE PINAFORE

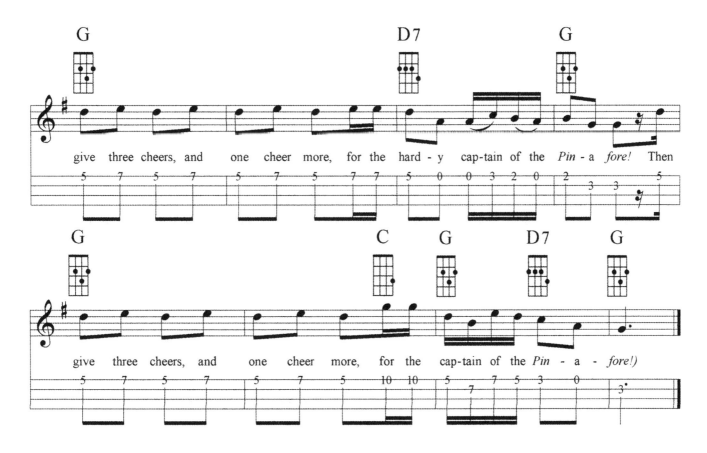

give three cheers, and one cheer more, for the hard - y cap-tain of the *Pin - a fore!* Then

give three cheers, and one cheer more, for the cap-tain of the *Pin - a - fore!*)

The CAPTAIN and SWEET LITTLE BUTTERCUP.
BUTTERCUP: "How sweetly he carols forth his melody to the unconscious moon."

H.M.S. PINAFORE

FROM THE CAPTAIN TO THE CREW:

2. I do my best to satisfy you all!
    (And with you we're quite content.)
    You're exceedingly polite, and I think it only right
    To return the compliment.
    Bad language or abuse, I never, never use,
    Whatever the emergency;
    Though "bother it" I may occasionally say,
    I never use a big, big D!
    (Then give three cheers, and then one more,
    For the well-bred Captain of the Pinafore!
    Then give three cheers, and then one more,
    For the Captain of the Pinafore!

I'm called Little Buttercup

Ukulele tuning: gCEA

GILBERT & SULLIVAN

THE SONGS OF GILBERT & SULLIVAN FOR UKULELE

Little Buttercup

LITTLE BUTTERCUP

LITTLE BUTTERCUP

THE SONGS OF GILBERT & SULLIVAN FOR UKULELE

I'VE GOT A LITTLE LIST

Ukulele tuning: gCEA

GILBERT & SULLIVAN

1.As some day it may hap - pen that a vic - tim must be found, I've got a lit - tle list, I've got a lit - tle list, of so - ci - e - ty of - fend - ers who might

I'VE GOT A LITTLE LIST

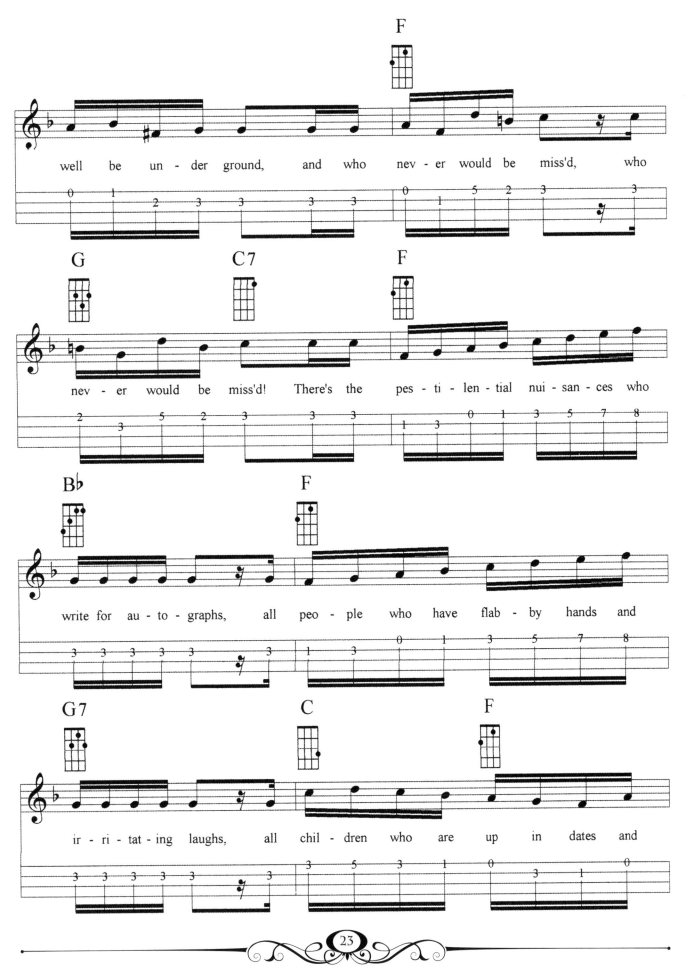

I'VE GOT A LITTLE LIST

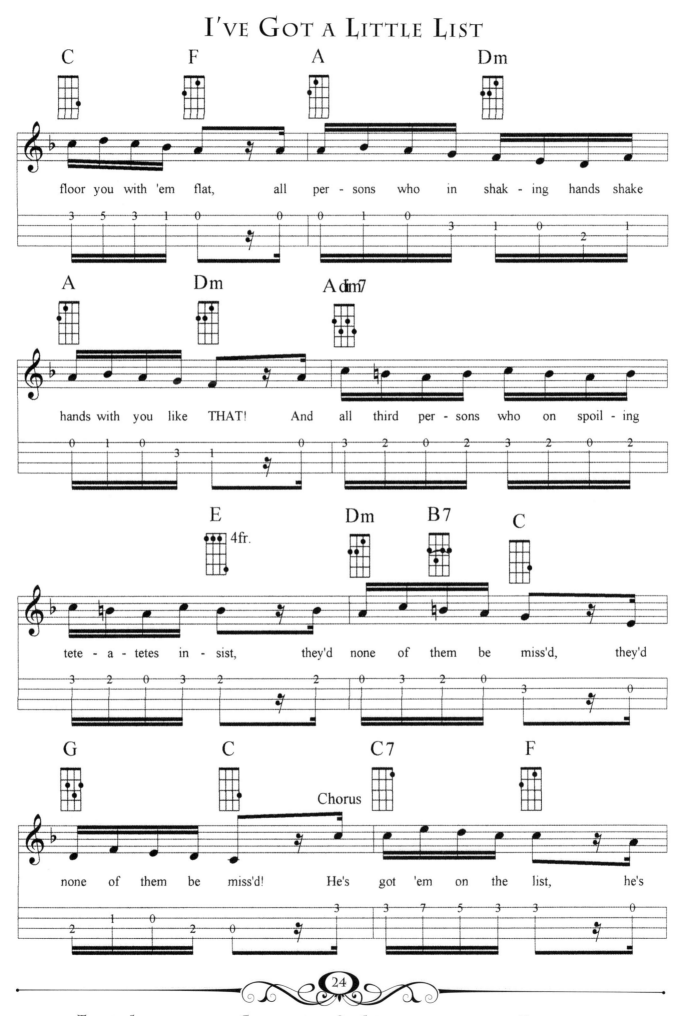

I'VE GOT A LITTLE LIST

got 'em on the list, and they'll _____ none of 'em be miss'd.

2. There's the banjo serenader and the others of his race,
   And the piano organist, I've got him on the list!
   And the people who eat peppermint and puff it in your face,
   They never would be miss'd, they never would be miss'd!
   Then the idiot who praises with enthusiastic tone,
   All centuries but this and ev'ry country but his own;
   And the lady from the provinces, who dresses like a guy,
   And who "doesn't think she dances, but would rather like to try,"
   And that singular anomaly, the lady novelist,
   I don't think she'd be missed, I'm sure she'd not be miss'd!
   He's got her on the list, he's got her on the list,
   And I don't think she'd be miss'd, I'm sure she'll not be miss'd.

3. And that Nisi Prius nuisance, who just now is rather rife,
   The Judicial humorist, I've got him on the list!
   All funny fellows, comic men and clowns of private life,
   They'd none of 'em be missed, they'd none of 'em be miss'd!
   And apologetic statesmen of a compromising kind,
   Such as What-d'ye-call-him, Thing-'em-bob, and likewise Never-mind,
   And 'St-'st-'st and What's-his-name, and also You-know-who,
   The task of filling up the blanks I'd rather leave to you.
   But it really doesn't matter whom you put upon the list,
   For they'd none of 'em be miss'd, they'd none of 'em be miss'd!
   You may put 'em on the list, you may put 'em on the list,
   And they'll none of 'em be miss'd, they'll none of 'em be miss'd!

IF YOU GIVE ME YOUR ATTENTION

Ukulele tuning: gCEA

GILBERT & SULLIVAN

If You Give Me Your Attention

2. To compliments inflated I've a withering reply;
    And vanity I always do my best to mortify;
    A charitable action I can skillfully dissect;
    And interested motives I'm delighted to detect;
    I know ev'ry body's income and what ev'rybody earns;
    And I'm careful to compare it with the income tax returns;
    But to benefit humanity however much I plan,
    Yet ev'ry body says I'm such a disagreeable man!
    And I can't think why!

3. I'm sure I'm not ascetic, I'm as pleasant as can be;
    You'll always find me ready with a crushing repartee;
    I've an irritating chuckle, I've a celebrated sneer;
    I've an entertaining snigger, I've a fascinating leer;
    To ev'rybody's prejudice I know a thing or two;
    I can tell a woman's age in half a minute, and I do.
    But although I try to make myself as pleasant as I can,
    Yet ev'rybody says I'm such a disagreeable man!
    And I can't think why! He can't think why! I can't think why!

MODEL OF A MODERN MAJOR GENERAL

Ukulele tuning: gCEA

GILBERT & SULLIVAN

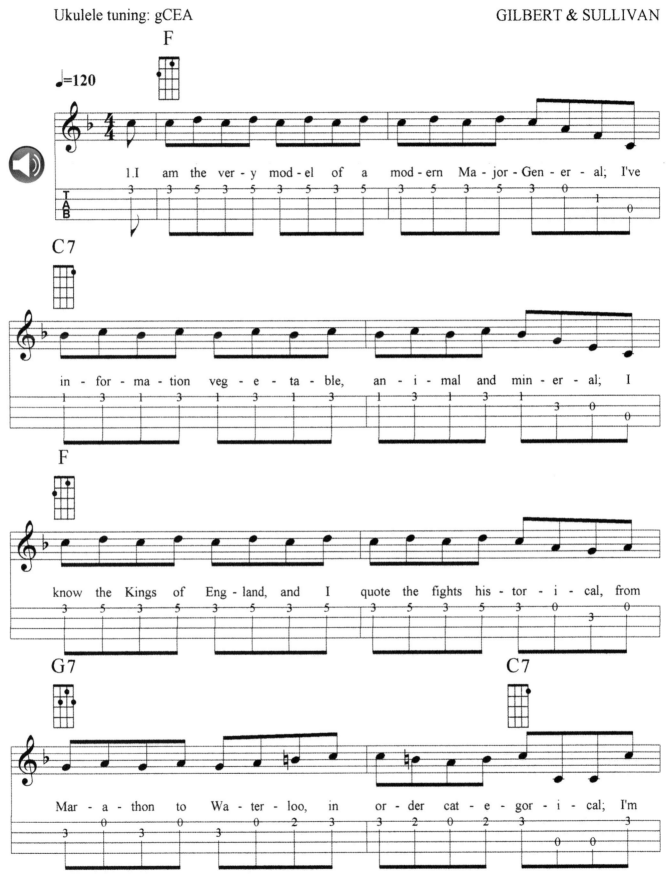

MODEL OF A MODERN MAJOR GENERAL

MODEL OF A MODERN MAJOR GENERAL

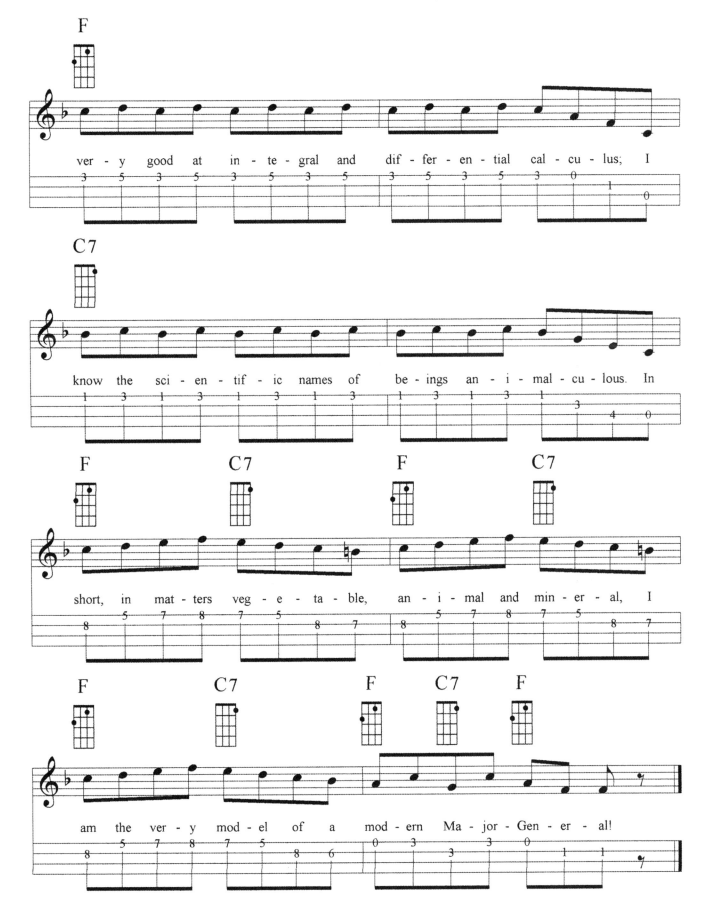

THE SONGS OF GILBERT & SULLIVAN FOR UKULELE

Model of a Modern Major General

2. I know our mythic history,
   King Arthur's and Sir Caradoc's;
   I answer hard acrostics,
   I've a pretty taste for a paradox;
   I quote in elegiacs all the crimes
   of Heliogabalus!
   In conics I can floor peculiarities parabolus.
   I can tell undoubted Raphaels
   From Gerard Dows and Zoffanies.
   I know the croaking chorus
   From the "Frogs" of Aristophanes!

Then I can hum a fugue of which
I've heard the music's din afore,
And whistle all the airs from that
Infernal nonsense "Pinafore."
Then I can write a washing bill
In Babylonic cuneiform,
And tell you every detail of
Caractacus's uniform.
In short, in matters vegetable,
Animal and mineral,
I am the very model of a
Modern Major-General!

Savoy Theatre, London, 1881

MY OBJECT ALL SUBLIME

Ukulele tuning: gCEA

GILBERT & SULLIVAN

OH, A PRIVATE BUFFOON

Ukulele tuning: gCEA

GILBERT & SULLIVAN

2. If you wish to succeed as a jester you'll need to consider each person's auric'lar:
    What is all right for B would quite scandalize C (for C is so very partic'lar!)
    And D may be dull, and E's very thick skull is as empty of brains as a ladle;
    While F is F sharp, and will cry with a carp that he's known your best joke from his cradle!
    When your humour they flout, you can't let yourself go, and it does put you out when a person says:
    "Oh, I have known that old joke from my cradle!"

OH, A PRIVATE BUFFOON

3. If your master is surly from getting up early (and tempers are short in the morning),
And inopportune joke is enough to provoke him to give you at once a month's warning.
Then if you refrain, he is at you again, for he likes to get value for money;
He'll ask then and there, with an insolent stare, "If you know that you're paid to be funny?"
It adds to the task of a merry man's place, when your principal asks, with a scowl on his face,
If you know that you're paid to be funny?

Oh, A Private Buffoon

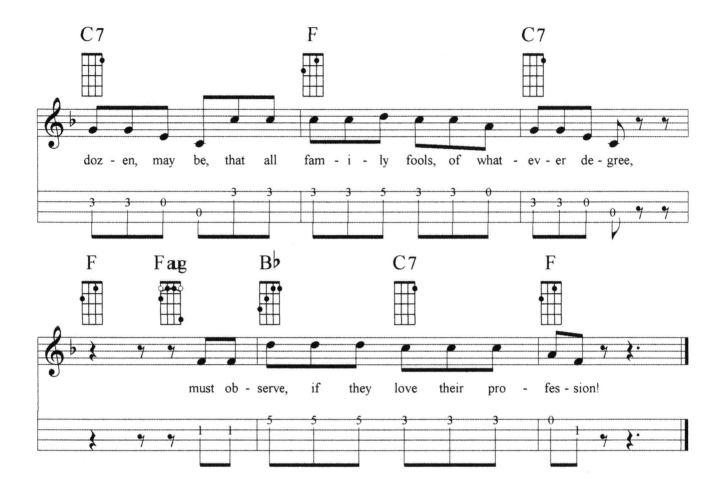

4. Comes a Bishop, maybe, or a solemn D.D., oh, beware of his anger provoking!
   Better not pull his hair, don't stick pins in his chair; he don't understand practical joking.
   If the jests that you crack have an orthodox smack, you may get a bland smile from these sages;
   But should they, by chance, be imported from France, half a crown is stopp'd out of your wages!
   It's a general rule, tho' your zeal it may quench, if the family fool tells a joke that's too French,
   Half a crown is stopp'd out of his wages!

5. Tho' your head it may rack with a bilious attack, and your senses with toothache you're losing,
   Don't be mopy and flat, they don't fine you for that, if youre properly quaint and amusing!
   Tho' your wife ran away with a soldier that day, and took with her your trifle of money;
   Bless your heart, they don't mind, they're exceedingly kind, they don't blame you as long as you're funny!
   It's a comfort to feel, if your partner should flit, tho' you suffer a deal, they don't mind it a bit;
   They don't blame you so long as you're funny!

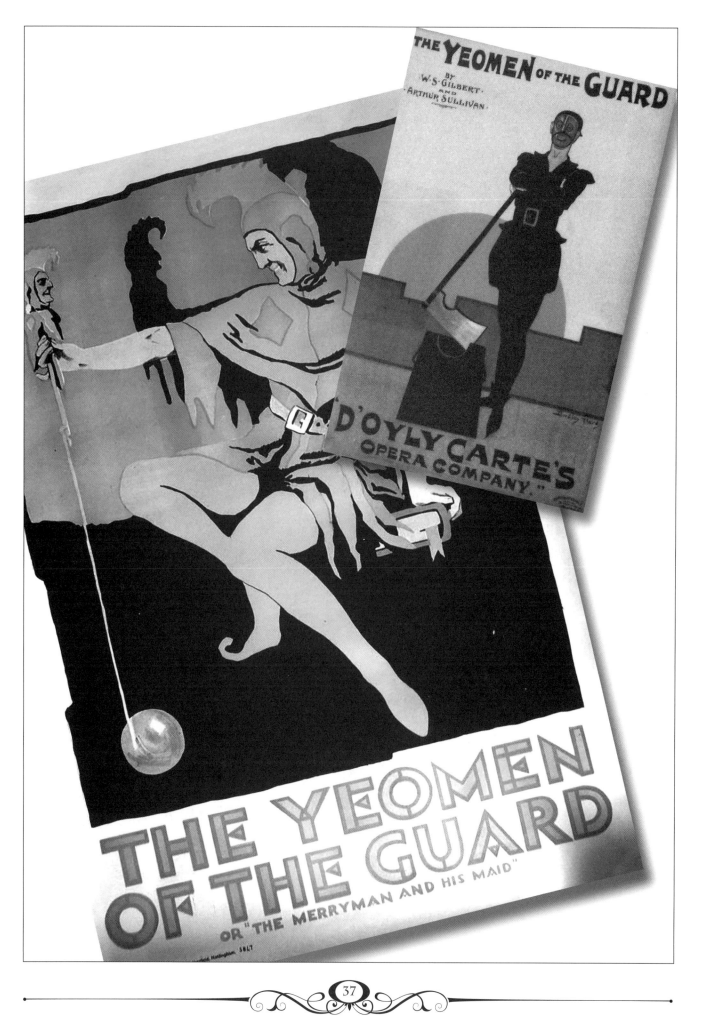

THE SONGS OF GILBERT & SULLIVAN FOR UKULELE

POOR WANDERING ONE

Ukulele tuning: gCEA

GILBERT & SULLIVAN

(Mabel) Poor wan-d'ring one! _____ Tho' thou hast sure - ly strayed,

take heart of grace, thy steps re - trace, poor wan - d'ring one! _____

Poor wan - d'ring one! _____ If such poor love as mine

can help thee find true peace of mind, why, take it, it _____ is thine!

Poor Wandering One

Taken From the County Jail
(from Behold the Lord High Executioner)

Ukulele tuning: gCEA

GILBERT & SULLIVAN

Taken From the County Jail

THE FLOWERS THAT BLOOM IN THE SPRING

Ukulele tuning: gCEA

GILBERT & SULLIVAN

FLOWERS THAT BLOOM

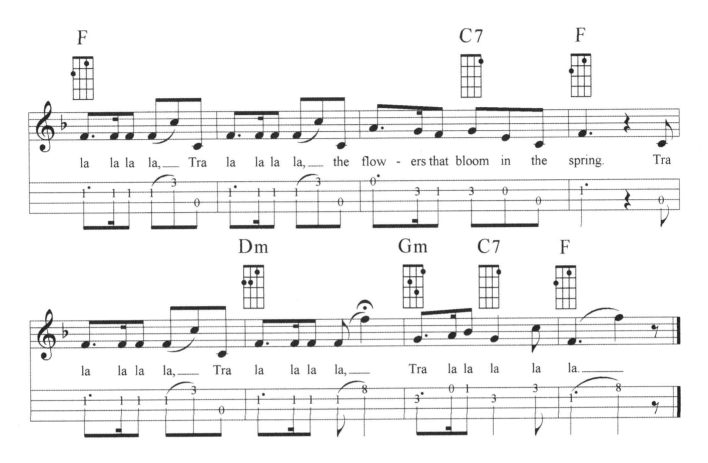

la   la la la,___ Tra   la   la la la,___ the flow - ers that bloom in   the   spring.   Tra

la   la la la,___ Tra   la   la la la,___ Tra la la la la la.___

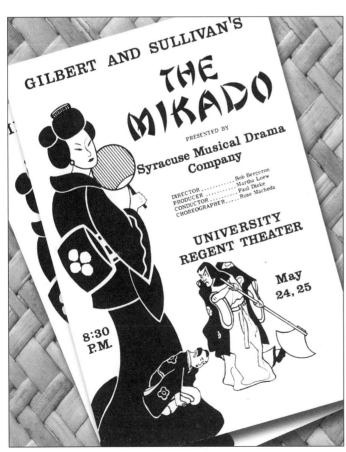

2. The flowers that bloom in the spring, Tra la,
    Have nothing to do with the case.
    I've got to take under my wing, Tra la,
    A most unattractive old thing, Tra la,
    With a caricature of a face,
    With a caricature of a face;
    And that's what I mean when I say, or I sing,
    "Oh, bother the flowers that bloom in the spring,"
    Tra la la la la, Tra la la la la,
    "Oh, bother the flowers of spring!"
    Tra la la la la, Tra la la la la,
    Tra la la la la, la!

The Moon and I

Ukulele tuning: gCEA

GILBERT & SULLIVAN

1. The sun, whose rays are all a - blaze with ev - er liv - ing glo - ry,

does not de - ny his maj - es - ty he scorns to tell a sto - ry!

He don't ex - claim, "I blush for shame, so kind - ly be in - dul - gent."

But, fierce and bold, in fie - ry gold, he glo - ries all ef - ful - gent!

THE MOON AND I

2. Observe his flame, that placid dame, the moon's Celestial Highness;
There's not a trace upon her face of diffidence or shyness:
She borrows light that, through the night, mankind my all acclaim her!
And truth to tell, she lights up well, so I, for one, don't blame her!
Ah, pray make no mistake, we are not shy; we're very wide awake,
The moon and I!

THERE IS BEAUTY
IN THE BELLOW OF THE BLAST

AS SUNG BY KATISHA & KO-KO

Ukulele tuning: gCEA

GILBERT & SULLIVAN

1.There is beau - ty in the bel - low of the blast, there is grand - eur in the growl - ing of the gale, there is e - lo - quent out-pour - ing when the li - on is a-roar - ing and the ti - ger is a-lash - ing of his tail! Yes, I

(Katisha)

(Ko-Ko)

THE SONGS OF GILBERT & SULLIVAN FOR UKULELE

THERE IS BEAUTY

like to see a ti - ger from the Con - go or the Ni - ger, and es -

pe - cial - ly when lash - ing of his tail! (Katisha) Vol - ca - noes have a splend - our that is

grim, and ____ earth - quakes on - ly ter - ri - fy the dolts, (Ko-Ko) but to

THE SONGS OF GILBERT & SULLIVAN FOR UKULELE

There is Beauty

THERE IS BEAUTY

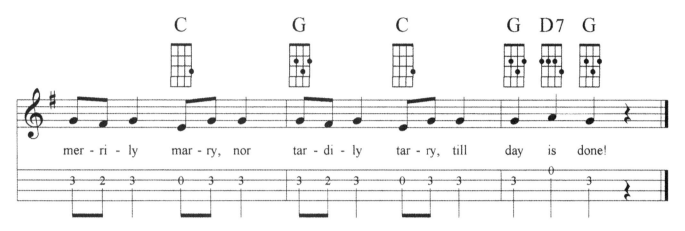

merri - ly mar - ry, nor tar - di - ly tar - ry, till day is done!

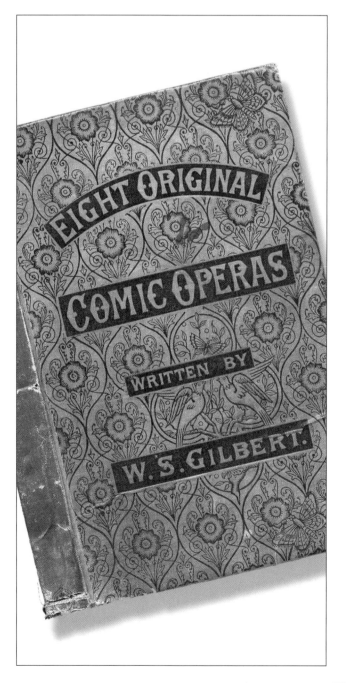

Ko-Ko:
2. There is beauty in extreme old age,
Do you fancy you are elderly enough?
Information I'm requesting
On a subject interesting:
Is a maiden all the better when she's tough?

Katisha:
Throughout this wide dominion
It's the general opinion
That she'll last a good deal longer when she's tough.

Both:
If that is so sing derry down derry,
It's evident, very, our tastes our one.
Away we'll go and merrily marry
Nor tardily tarry till day is done.

Tit-Willow

Ukulele tuning: gCEA

GILBERT & SULLIVAN

TIT-WILLOW

2. He slapped at his chest, as he sat on that bough,
   Singing "Willow, tit-willow, tit-willow!"
   And a cold perspiration bespangled his brow,
   Oh, Willow, tit-willow, tit-willow!
   He sobbed and he sighed, and a gurgle he gave,
   Then he plunged himself into the billowy wave,
   And an echo arose from the suicide's grave,
   "Oh, Willow, tit-willow, tit-willow!"

3. Now I feel just as sure as I'm sure that my name
   Isn't Willow, tit-willow, tit-willow,
   That 'twas blighted affection that made him exclaim,
   "Oh, Willow, tit-willow, tit-willow!"
   And if you remain callous and obdurate, I
   Shall perish as he did, and you will know why,
   Though I probably shall not exclaim as I die,
   "Oh Willow, tit-willow, tit-willow!"

THE SONGS OF GILBERT & SULLIVAN FOR UKULELE

WE SAIL THE OCEAN BLUE

Ukulele tuning: gCEA

GILBERT & SULLIVAN

We __ sail the o - cean blue, and our sau - cy ship's a beau - ty; we're

so - ber men and true, and at - ten - tive to our du - ty. When the

balls whis - tle free o'er the bright blue sea, we stand to our guns all __ day. When at

We Sail the Ocean Blue

an - chor we ride on the Ports-mouth tide, we've plen - ty of time for play. A-hoy! A-

hoy! The balls whis-tle free. A-hoy! A - hoy! O'er the bright blue sea, we stand to our

guns, to our guns all day._____ We_ sail the o - cean blue, and our

We Sail the Ocean Blue

THE SONGS OF GILBERT & SULLIVAN FOR UKULELE

WHEN I, GOOD FRIENDS,
WAS CALLED TO THE BAR

Ukulele tuning: gCEA

GILBERT & SULLIVAN

1.When I, good friends, was call'd to the bar, I'd an ap-pe-tite fresh and heart-y: but

I was as man-y young bar-ris-ters are, an im-pe-cu-ni-ous par-ty. I'd a

swal-low tail coat of a beau-ti-ful blue, a brief which I bought of a boob-y; a

Gilbert & Sullivan Society
production of "Trial by Jury"
Sydney, Australia, 1937

56

WHEN I, GOOD FRIENDS...

THE SONGS OF GILBERT & SULLIVAN FOR UKULELE

WHEN I, GOOD FRIENDS...

good   Judge   too!   For   good   Judge   too!

2. In Westminster Hall I danc'd a dance, like a semi-despondent fury:
   For I thou't I should never hit on a chance, of addressing a British jury.
   But I soon got tired of third-class journeys and dinners of bread and water;
   So I fell in love with a rich attorney's elderly, ugly daughter.
   > *Chorus:* So he fell in love with a rich attorney's elderly, ugly daughter.

3. The rich attorney, he jumped for joy, and replied to my fond professions:
   "You shall reap the reward of you pluck, my boy, at the Bailey and Middlesex Sessions.
   You'll soon get used to her looks," said he, "And a very nice girl you'll find her;
   She may very well pass for forty-three, in the dusk with a light behind her."
   > *Chorus:* She has often been taken for forty-three, in the dusk, with a light behind her.

4. The rich attorney was good as his word, the briefs came trooping gaily,
   And every day my voice was heard, at the Sessions or ancient Bailey.
   All thieves, who could my fees afford, relied on my orations,
   And many a burglar I've restored to his friends and his relations.
   > *Chorus:* And many a burglar he's restored to his friends and his relations.

5. At length I became as rich as the Gurneys, an incubus then I thought her,
   So I threw over that rich attorney's elderly, ugly daughter.
   The rich attorney my character high tried vainly to disparage,
   And now, if you please, I'm ready to try this Breach of Promise marriage.
   > *Chorus:* And now, if you please, he's ready to try this Breach of Promise marriage.

The Songs of Gilbert & Sullivan for Ukulele

When I Was a Lad

Ukulele tuning: gCEA

GILBERT & SULLIVAN

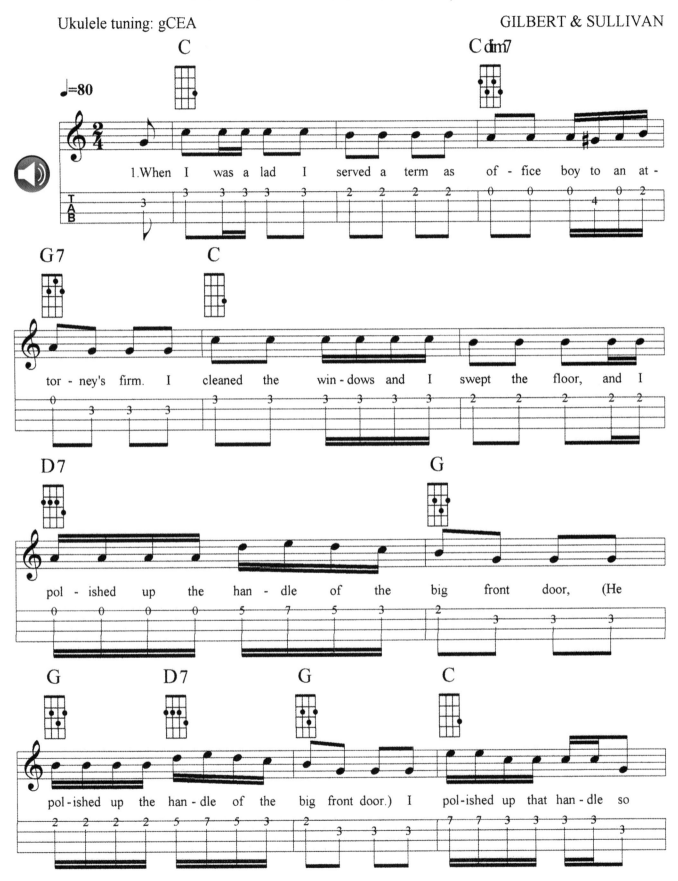

1.When I was a lad I served a term as of-fice boy to an at-tor-ney's firm. I cleaned the win-dows and I swept the floor, and I pol-ished up the han-dle of the big front door, (He pol-ished up the han-dle of the big front door.) I pol-ished up that han-dle so

THE SONGS OF GILBERT & SULLIVAN FOR UKULELE

WHEN I WAS A LAD

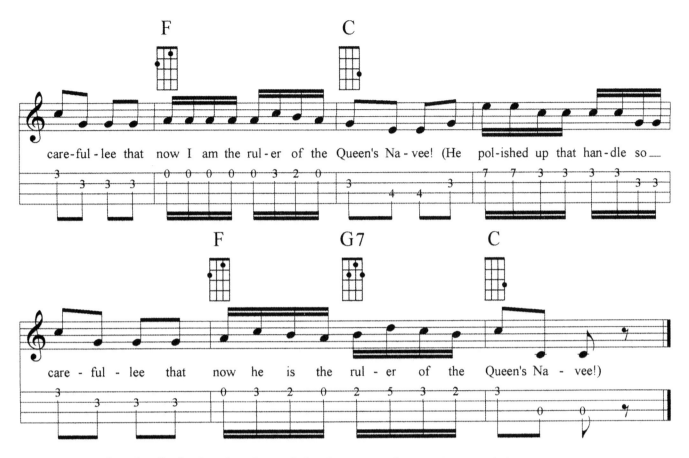

care-ful-lee that now I am the rul-er of the Queen's Na-vee! (He pol-ished up that han-dle so___

care-ful-lee that now he is the rul-er of the Queen's Na-vee!)

2. As office boy I made such a mark that they gave me the post of a junior clerk.
I served the writs with a smile so bland, and I copied all the letters in a big round hand.
(He copied all the letters in a big round hand.)
I copied all the letters in a hand so free that now I am the ruler of the Queen's Navee!
(He copied all the letters in a hand so free that now he is the ruler of the Queen's Navee!)

3. In serving writs I made such a name that an articled clerk I soon became;
I wore clean collars and a brand new suit for the pass examination at the Institute.
(For the pass examination at the Institute.)
That pass examination did so well for me that now I am the ruler of the Queen's Navee!
(That pass examination did so well for him that now he is the ruler of the Queen's Navee!)

4. Of legal knowledge I acquired such a grip that they took me into the partnership.
And that junior partnership, I ween, was the only ship I ever had seen.
(Was the only ship he ever had seen.)
But that kind of ship so suited me that now I am the ruler of the Queen's Navee!
(But that kind of partnership so suited him that now he is the ruler of the Queen's Navee!)

5. I grew so rich that I was sent by a pocket borough into Parliament.
I always voted at my party's call, and I never thought of thinking for myself at all.
(He never thought of thinking for himself at all.)
I thought so little, they rewarded me by making me the ruler of the Queen's Navee!
(He thought so little they rewarded him by making him the ruler of the Queen's Navee!)

6. Now landsmen all, whoever you may be, if you want to rise to the top of the tree,
If your soul isn't fettered to an office stool, be careful to be guided by this golden rule,
(Be careful to be guided by this golden rule.)
Stick close to your desks and never go to sea, and you all may be rulers of the Queen's Navee!
(Stick close to your desks and never go to sea, and you all may be rulers of the Queen's Navee!)

WHEN I WENT TO THE BAR

Ukulele tuning: gCEA

GILBERT & SULLIVAN

Lyrics:
1.When I went to the Bar as a ver-y young man (Said I to my-self, said I), I'll work on a new and o-rig-i-nal plan (Said I to my-self, said I), I'll____ nev-er as-sume that a rogue or a thief is a gen-tle-man worth-y im-

WHEN I WENT TO THE BAR

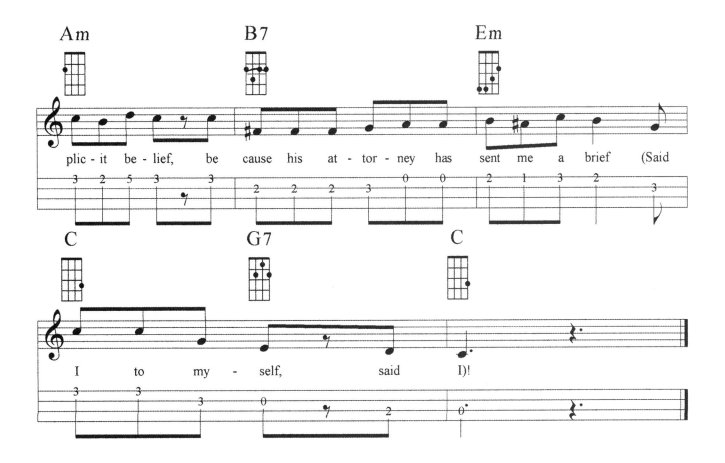

plic - it be - lief, be cause his at - tor - ney has sent me a brief (Said

I to my - self, said I)!

2. Ere I go into court I will read my brief through
   (Said I to myself, said I),
   And I'll never take work I'm unable to do
   (Said I to myself, said I),
   My learned profession I'll never disgrace
   By taking a fee with a grin on my face,
   When I haven't been there to attend to the case
   (Said I to myself, said I)!

3. I'll never throw dust in a jurymans's eyes
   (Said I to myself, said I),
   Or hoodwink a judge who is not overwise
   (Said I to myself, said I),
   Or assume that the witnesses summoned in force
   In Exchequer, Queen's Benchy, Common Please, or Divorce,
   Have perjur'd themselves as a matter of course
   Said I to myself, said I)!

4. In other professions in which men engage,
   (Said I to myself, said I),
   The Army, the Navy, the Church and the Stage,
   (Said I to myself, said I),
   Professional license, if carried too far,
   Your chance of promotion will certainly mar,
   And I fancy the fule might apply to the Bar,
   (Said I to myself, said I)!

WHEN YOU'RE LYING AWAKE

Ukulele tuning: gCEA

GILBERT & SULLIVAN

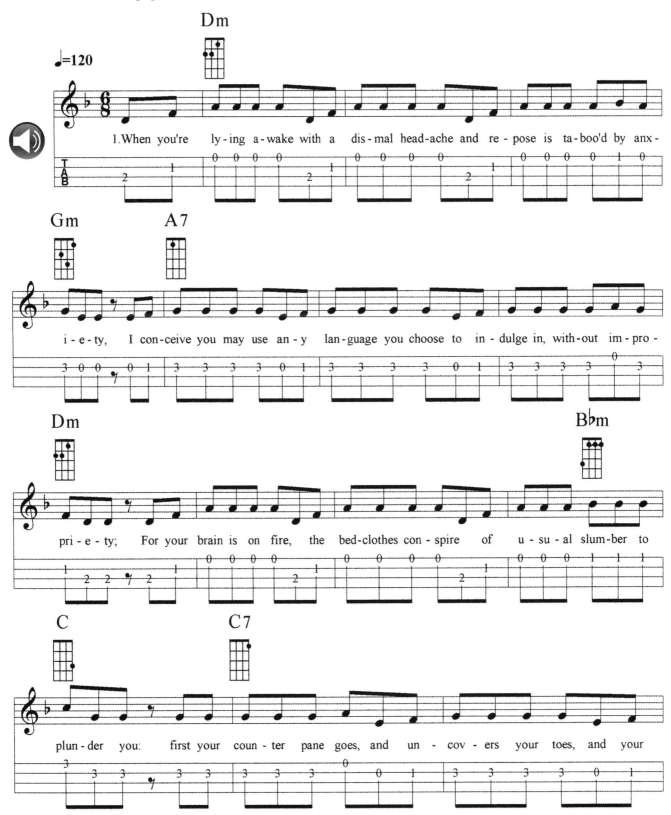

1.When you're ly-ing a-wake with a dis-mal head-ache and re-pose is ta-boo'd by anx-i-e-ty, I con-ceive you may use an-y lan-guage you choose to in-dulge in, with-out im-pro-pri-e-ty; For your brain is on fire, the bed-clothes con-spire of u-su-al slum-ber to plun-der you: first your coun-ter pane goes, and un-cov-ers your toes, and your

When You're Lying Awake

When You're Lying Awake

WHEN YOU'RE LYING AWAKE

"Iolanthe" by William Russell Flint

2. For you dream you are crossing the Channel and tossing
    Like mad in a steamer from Harwich,
    Which is something between a large bathing machine,
    And a very small second-class carriage;
    And you're giving a treat (penny ice and cold meat)
    To a party of friends and relations;
    They're a ravenous horde, and they all come aboard
    At Sloane Square and South Kensington Stations.
    And bound on that journey you find your attorney
    (Who started that morning from Devon);
    He's a bit undersized, and you don't feel surpris'd
    When he tells you he's only eleven.
    Well, you're driving like mad with this singular lad,
    By the by the ship's now a four wheeler.
    And you're playing round games, and he calls you bad names
    When you tell him that "ties pay the dealer."
    But this you can't stand, so you throw up your hand,
    And you find that you're cold as an icicle,
    In your shirt and your socks (the black silk with gold clocks)
    Crossing Salisbury plain on a bicycle.

3. And he and the crew are on bicycles too
    Which they somehow or other invested in,
    And he's telling the tars all the particulars
    Of the company he's interested in;
    It's a scheme of devices to get at low prices
    All goods from cough mixtures to cables;
    (Which tickles the sailors) by treating retailers
    As tho' they were all vegetables.
    You get a good spadesman to plant a small tradesman
    (First take off his boots with a boot-tree;)
    And his legs will take root! and his fingers will shoot,
    And they'll blossom and spread like a fruit tree.
    From the green-grocer tree you get grapes and green peas,
    Cauliflowers, pineapples and cranberries!
    While the pastry cook plant cherry brandy will grant,
    Apple puffs and three-comers and banberries.
    The shares are a penny and ever so many
    Are taken by Rothschild and Baring,
    And just as a few are allotted to you,
    You awake with a shudder despairing.

CONCLUSION (MUSIC NOT INCLUDED)

You're a regular wreck, with a crick in your neck;
And no wonder you snore, for your head's on the floor,
And you're needles and pins from your soles to your shins;
And your flesh is a-creep, for your left leg's a-sleep,
And you've cramp is your toes, and a fly on your nose,
And some fluff in your lung, and a feverish tongue,
And a thirst that's intense, and a general sense
That you haven't been sleeping in clover!
But the darkness has passed, and it's daylight at last,
And the night has been long, ditto, ditto, my song;
And thank goodness, they're both of them over!

THE SONGS OF GILBERT & SULLIVAN FOR UKULELE

Whene'er I Spoke

Ukulele tuning: gCEA

GILBERT & SULLIVAN

1.When - e'er I spoke, sar - cas - tic joke, re - plete with mal - ice spite - ful, this

peo - ple mild po - lite - ly smil'd, and vo - ted me de - light - ful! Now

when a wight sits up all night, ill - na - tur'd jokes de - vi - sing, and

all his wiles are met with smiles, it's hard, there's no dis - guis - ing! Ah!_____ Oh,

WHENE'ER I SPOKE

don't the days seem dark and long, when all goes right and noth-ing goes wrong, and

isn't your life ex - treme - ly flat with noth-ing what - ev - er to_____ ble at! Oh!

isn't your life ex - treme - ly flat with noth-ing what - ev - er to grum - ble at.

2. When German bands from music stands
   Play'd Wagner imperfectly,
   I bade them go, they didn't say no,
   But off they went directly!
   The organ boys, they stopped their noise,
   With readiness surprising,
   And grinning herds of hurdy-gurds
   Retired apologising.
   Ah! Don't the days seem lank and long,
   When all goes right and nothing goes wrong,
   And isn't your life extremely flat
   With nothing whatever to grumble at!
   Chorus: Oh! Isn't your life extremely flat
               With nothing whatever to grumble at!

3. I offer'd gold in sums untold
   To all who'd contradict me,·
   I said I'd pay a pound a day
   To anyone who kicked me.
   I brib'd with toys great vulgar boys
   to utter something spiteful,
   But, bless you, no! they would be so
   Confoundedly politeful!
   Ah! In short, these aggravating lads,
   They tickly my tastes, they feed my fads,
   They give me this and they give me that,
   And I've nothing whatever to grumble at!
   Chorus: Oh! Isn't your life extremely flat
               With nothing whatever to grumble at!

THE SONGS OF GILBERT & SULLIVAN FOR UKULELE

More Great Ukulele Books from Centerstream...

More Great Books from Dick Sheridan...

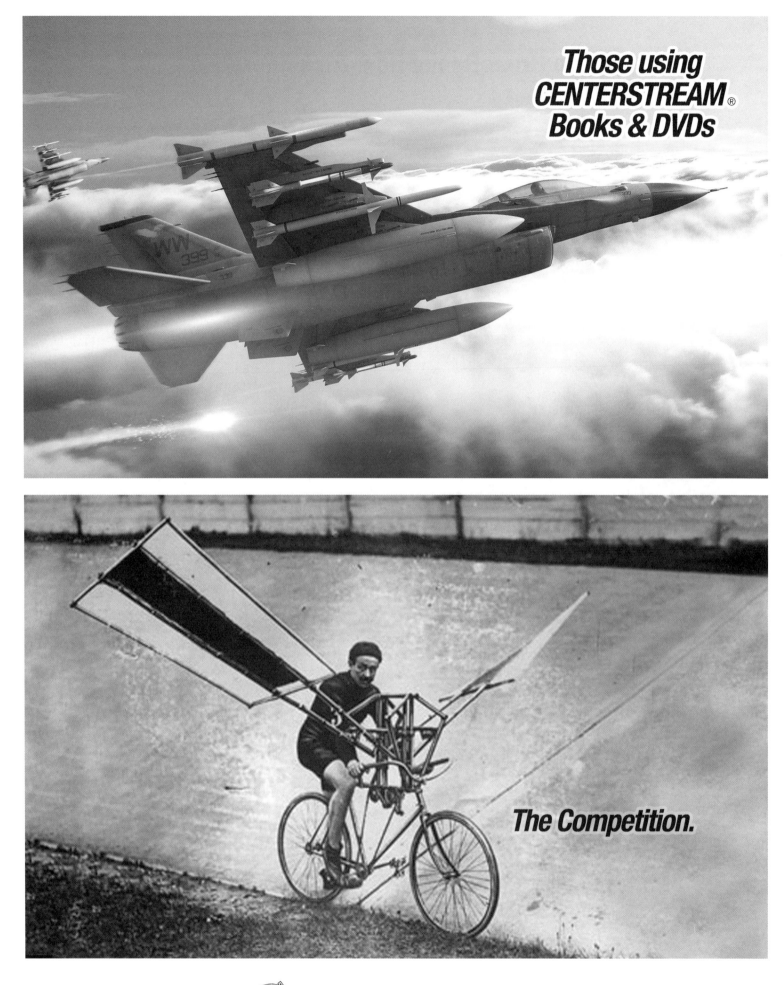